Minia

Knitting Patterns for Christmas Tree Decorations
By Betty Lampen
the author of "Miniature Sweaters" and "Sweaters for Teddy Bears"

CONTENTS

Instructions................................Inside Front Cover
Basic Pattern...2
Africa..3
Garden..4
Knave..5
Gnome..6
Confetti...7
Color Photos of Pullovers.....................................8-9
Teddy Bear & Roulette..10
House & Car...11
Puzzle & Stripe Front...12
College & Line 'n Dots...13
Love & Heart...14
Opposites Attract & Lattice..................................15
Clothes Line Yoke Pullover Pattern......................16
Splash & Jewel.........................Inside Back Cover

© 1992 Betty Lampen Dept. 2, 2930 Jackson St. San Francisco, CA 94115-1007
Printed by Haskin Press, S.F., CA • Photographer – Moulin Studios

Basic Pattern for Pullovers with Sleeves
(except Yoke sweaters)

Body   With size 0 knitting needles
Cast on 32 stitches. Rib 4 rows, K1 P1.
Change to Size 3 needles.
Knit 10 rows stockinette stitch (knit 1 row, purl 1 row).
Divide knitting, 16 sts for front.
Put 16 sts for back on separate needle.

Front   On 16 sts knit 4 rows stockinette
Shoulders: K 4 sts for 4 rows. Cast off.*
Cast off center 8 sts.*
Knit last 4 sts 4 rows stockinette. Cast off.*

Back   On 2nd needle of 16 sts knit 8 rows stockinette. Cast off.*
With tapestry needle sew shoulder sts to back piece.

Neck   With Size 0 needles (4 sock needles) pick up 24 sts around neck.
(8 in front, 4 on 1st shoulder, 8 in back, 4 on last shoulder.)
Rib 2 rows, K1 P1. Cast off in ribbing.

Sleeves   With Size 0 needles cast on 12 sts. Rib 4 rows, K1 P1.
Change to Size 3 needles.
Knit 8 rows stockinette.
Rows 9 and 10 – decrease 1 st at beginning and end of both rows (8 sts left on needle).
Cast off last 8 sts.

Finish   Carefully sew in sleeves first. Then side seams and sleeve seams, with very flat st.

* Note   To have a very smooth finish do not cast off.
Weave back and front-shoulder sts together.

Use back and front 8 center sts in neck ribbing.

As these sweaters are just for decoration, gather all yarns inside the sweater, tie them in a firm neat bunch and cut off the ends so that they do not show below the sweater.

Africa

Basic Pattern Instructions Page 2

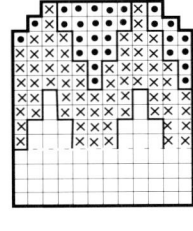
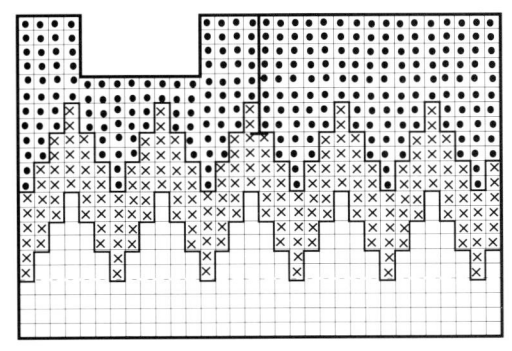
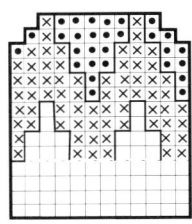

● = Yellow   X = Red   □ = Black

See Centerfold

Garden
Basic Pattern Instructions Page 2

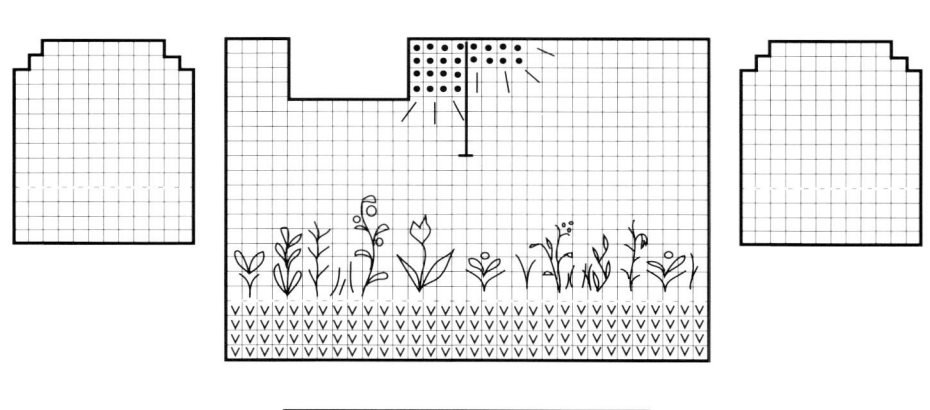

● = Yellow V = Green □ = Blue

Embroider green grasses & different color for flowers, yellow for sun rays.
See Centerfold

Knave

Basic Pattern Instructions Page 2

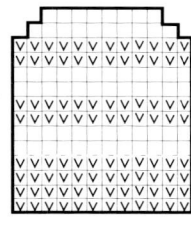
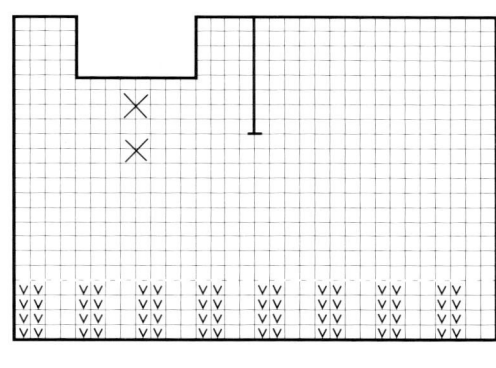
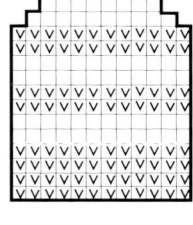

To begin: Cast on 32 sts as follows:
Cast on 2 sts green, 2 sts white across.
Continue in ribbing in those two
colors, for 3 more rows.

V = Green
2 Large X's embroider Red
Neck: Pick up 24 sts,
Cast off in ribbing
on 1st row.

See Centerfold

Gnome
Basic Pattern Instructions Page 2

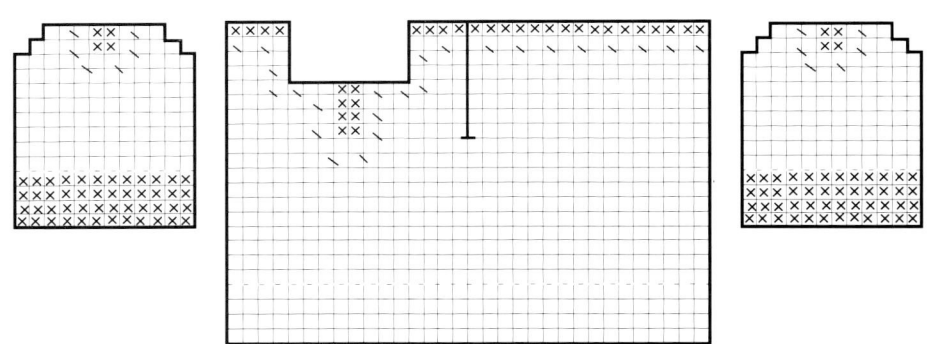

X = Red   Background White
\ = Tiny stitches, embroider in Red
See Centerfold

Confetti

Basic Pattern Instructions Page 2

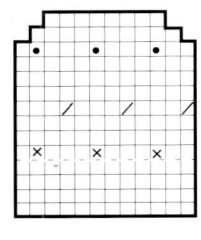
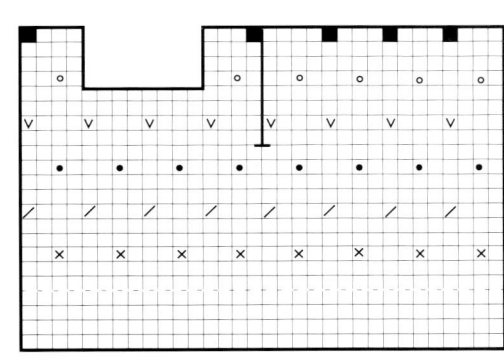
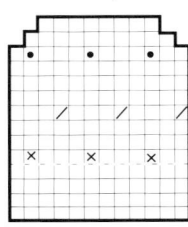

X = Red / = Orange
● = Yellow V = Green
○ = Blue ■ = Purple

See Centerfold

Teddy Bear

Basic Pattern Instructions Page 2

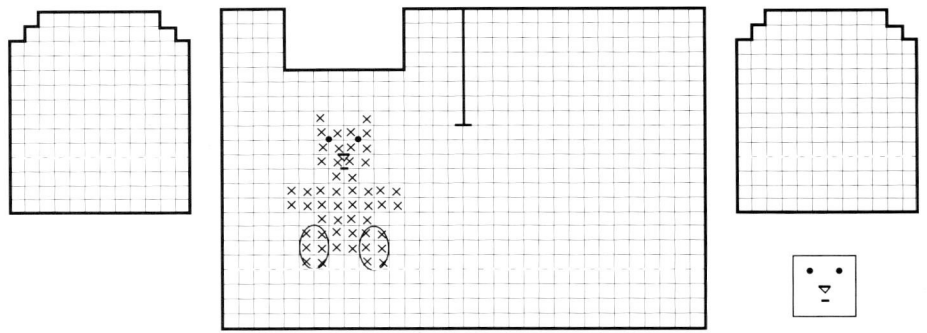

X = Brown
Background Light Blue
Circle feet with same brown
yarn and stitch down.
See Centerfold

With Black Thread
Eyes = French Knots
Nose = Black
Mouth = Black Embroider

Roulette

Basic Pattern Instructions Page 2

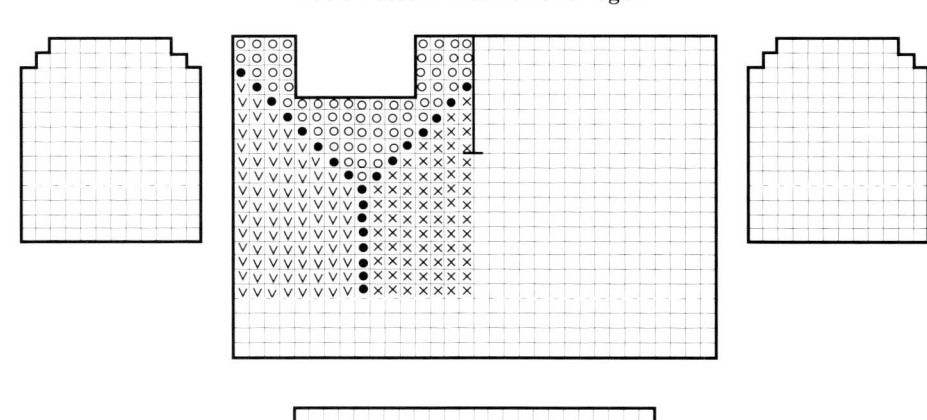

O = Yellow   V = Green
X = Red   • = Purple
See Centerfold

House

Basic Pattern Instructions Page 2

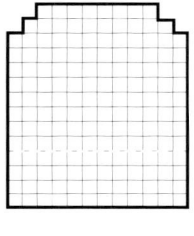 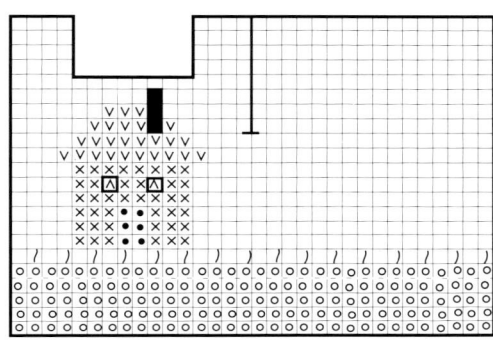 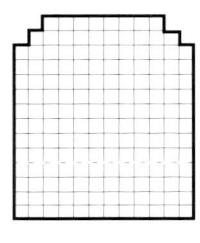

X = Red • = Black
V = Grey O = Green
Chimney = Red. Background = White
Embroider Door, Windows & Grass last.
See Centerfold

Car

Basic Pattern Instructions Page 2

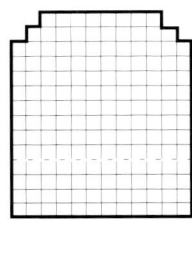 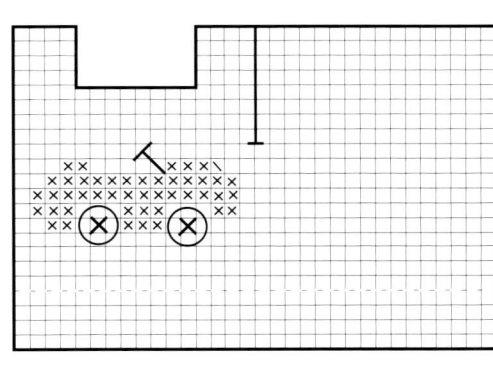 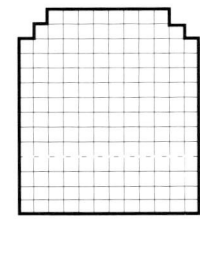

X = Red
Background White
Two 7/16th Blue Buttons for Wheels
Embroider Black Yarn for Steering Wheel.
See Centerfold

Puzzle

Basic Pattern Instructions Page 2

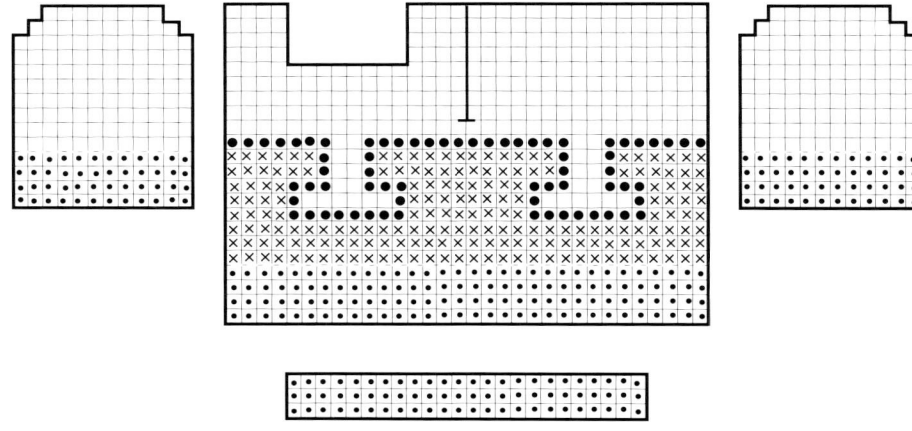

• = Black   X = Orange   ☐ = White
See Centerfold

Stripe Front

Basic Pattern Instructions Page 2

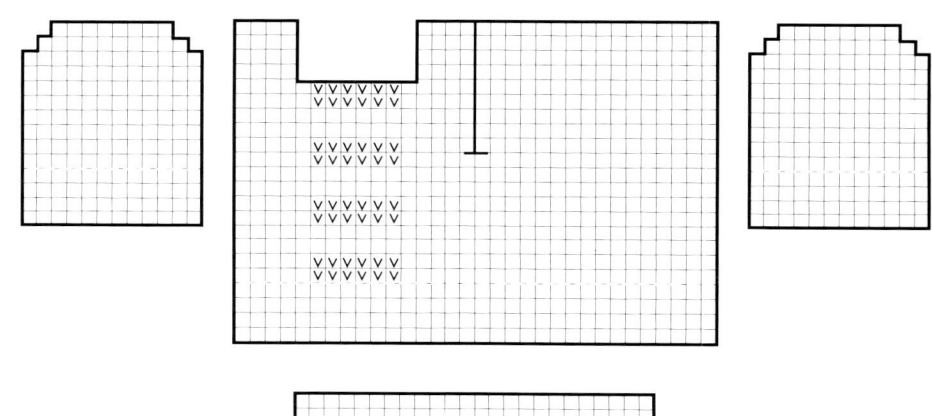

Stripe Front = White. Background = Red
See Centerfold

College

Basic Pattern Instructions Page 2

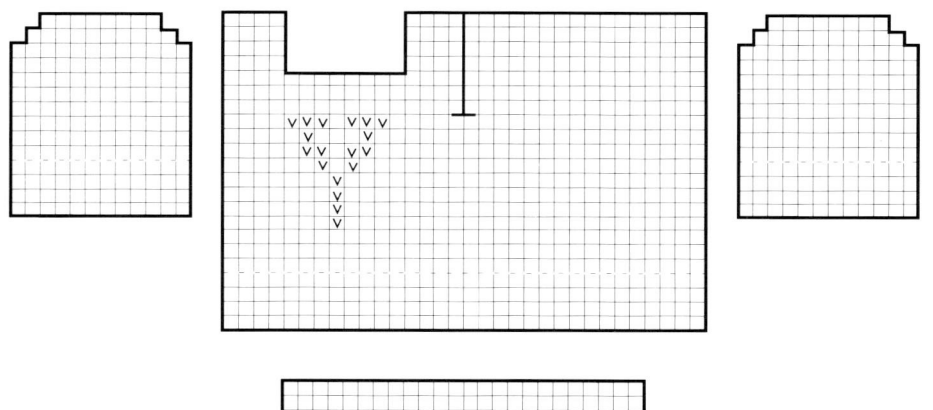

V = Blue   Background White
OR YOUR favorite logo (school, football or baseball team, etc...)
See Centerfold

Lines 'n Dots

Basic Pattern Instructions Page 2

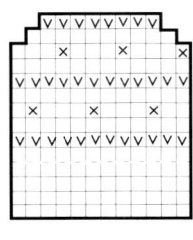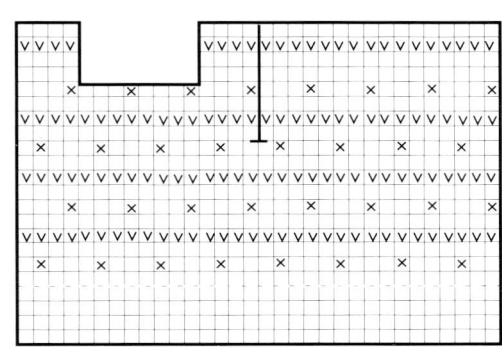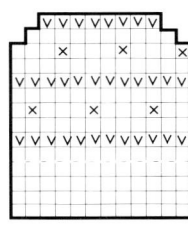

V = Blue   X = Red   Background White
See Centerfold

Love

Basic Pattern Instructions Page 2

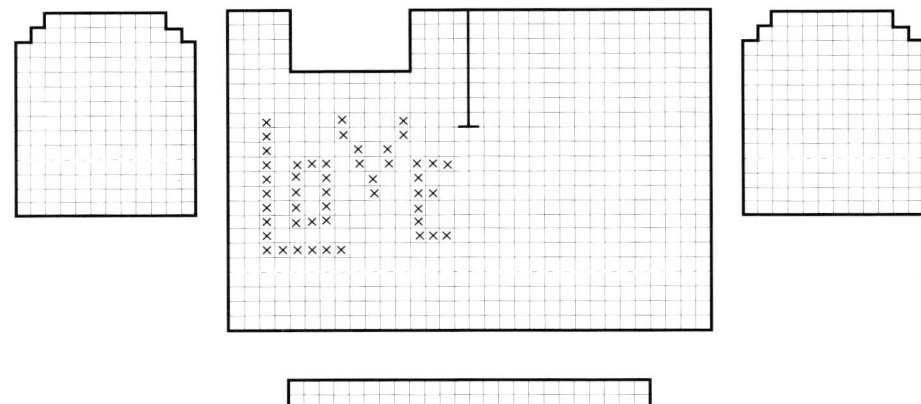

X = Blue   Background = White
See Centerfold

Heart

Basic Pattern Instructions Page 2

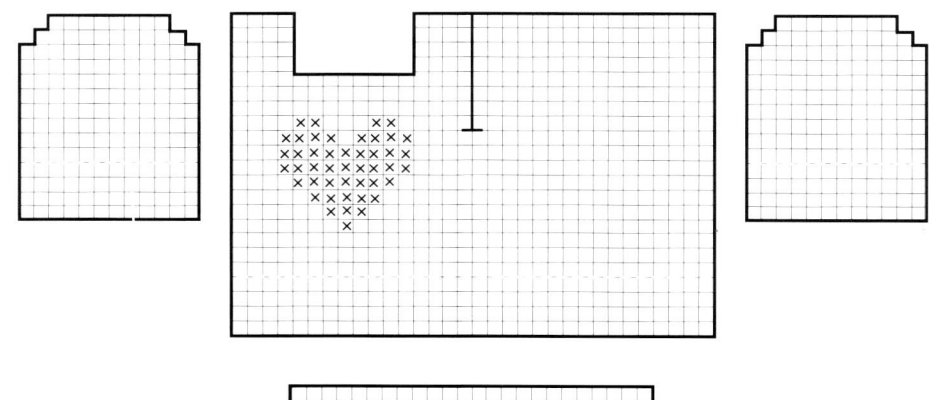

X = Red   Background = White
See Centerfold

Opposites Attract

Basic Pattern Instructions Page 2

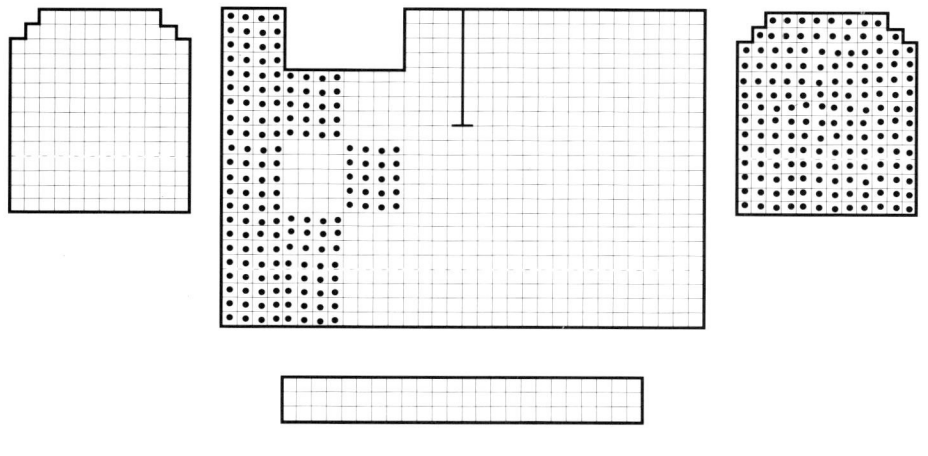

● = Yellow   □ = Navy Blue
See Centerfold

Lattice

Basic Pattern Instructions Page 2

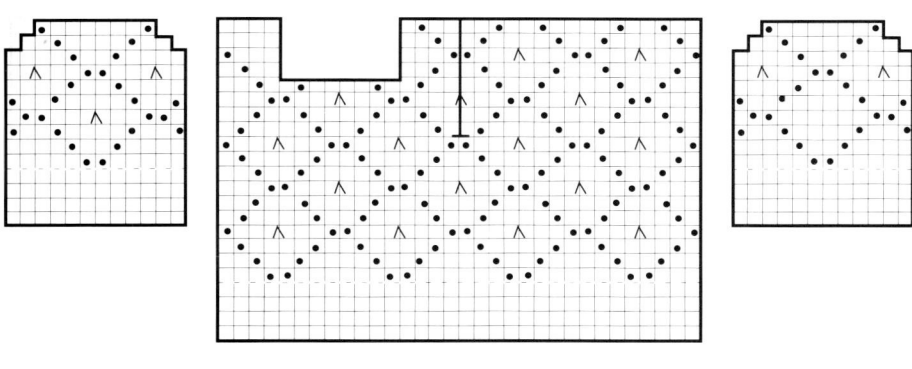

● = Black   Background = Pink   ∧ = Red, Embroider last
Stitch V upside-down
See Centerfold

CLOTHES LINE YOKE PULLOVER PATTERN

Body   With Size 0 needle cast on 16 sts.
Rib 3 rows, K1 P1.
Change to Size 3 needles.
Knit 10 rows Stockinette.
Cut yarn. Leave on needle.

Knit 2nd piece as above.
Cut Yarn. Leave on needle.

Sleeves   With Size 0 needle cast on 12 sts.
Rib 3 rows, K1 P1.
Change to Size 3 needles.
Knit 8 rows Stockinette.
Cut yarn. Leave on needle.

Knit 2nd sleeve.
Cut yarn. Leave on needle.

Yoke   With one Size 3 needle join all 4 pieces.
(See diagram on opposite page).
Body, sleeve, body, sleeve IN THAT ORDER. (56 sts.)
Start yoke pattern on opposite page.
Stockinette rows 1 through 7.
Ending with 24 sts.

Neck   Change to Size 0 needles on 24 sts.
Rib 2 rows, K1 P1
Cast off in ribbing.

Finish   Sew flat seam up yoke first.
Then sew body, sleeves and neck.
Gather all yarns inside sweater,
tie firmly and trim so it is not
visible on outside of sweater.